T0196565

Pain No More
Tooo

Shug

 www.trafford.com

North America & international
toll-free: 1 888 232 4444 (USA & Canada)
phone: 250 383 6864 ♦ fax: 812 355 4082

Contents

Dedication vii

Acknowledgements..ix

Introduction By Eather Mitchell xi

Chapter 1   Another New Start? 1

Chapter 2   The Woman with the Stupid Smile 4

Chapter 3   Nuclear Plant 7

Chapter 4   Greyhound 1980..12

Chapter 5   Christmas Eve 1980 17

Chapter 6   Body Search 22

Chapter 7   Naptime, Before Work 27

Chapter 8   Being Accused 32

Chapter 9   Cheerleader Coach 36

Chapter 10 Moving Again 41

Chapter 11 Who's sleeping in Shug's Bed?.......................................49

Chapter 12 He's Baaaccckkkkkk!..55

Chapter 13 Free at Last..61

Dedication

I would like to dedicate this book to GOD who is first and foremost in my life, and without HIM none of this would have been possible.

To my two children who lived this nightmare with me. To my grandchildren who I love dearly.

Lastly, to all the women who are living in an abusive relationship, there is hope out there for you. This book is written as a testament to encourage you all to know, that no matter how bad things get, you can draw strength and gain the courage to get out and live an abuse free life.

Acknowledgements

First and far most I want to Thank God for giving me the strength and courage to endure my past and survive. Pastor Leona Cromartie and Brother John Cromartie her companion, Pastor Luel Campbell, Evangelist Barbara Campbell and Wendell Campbell, always keeping me in their prayers. New Beginnings and True Vine Family. The Bladen County Law Enforcement, Clerks, Judges, District Attorneys Office, Probation Office Staff, Magistrates, Attorneys, and all of Bladen County Library Staff.

To my big brother Peter, wife Diane and daughter, Laverne, Kammie, Gary, Keith, Eather Mitchell and daughters, Mwandishi Walker, Keisha Walker, Wanda Shipman and sons, Trevon and Michael, Ida Stocks, Karen George, Veronica and Lillian Lucas, Marcella Chappell, Cindy Edwards, and Robert Henry Jessup, Sonia Johnson daughter Sonisha McMillan, CSR Lawn Care Service Rodgers and Sharika Richardson, my good friend Arvis.

J.C., Ellen Gill, Leroy, Veronica, Reginald Darnell, and son R. J, Tatum, Ronald McLaughlin, Sophia Huff, Tiquan, Keshara and Otis. Cynthia, Peggy and Keith Newkirk, Michael, Paula Thomas, Datisha Montgomery, Valerie Sledge and their families. M&E Productions for Domestic Violence. The Red Hat Sisters of Bladen County North Carolina. Ms.Erin Smith of Bladen Journal who is always educating the community on domestic violence with her articles. The Great Cast of Why Me: Anthony and Jessica Thomas (Writer and Director) of Dirty Laundry and all the Great Cast.

Mrs. Doris Gwynn. Of Yanceyville. Rhonda Griffin of Bladen Online. To all of my SOAR Sisters, I love and miss dearly. Sam, Brandy, Sarah and Laura Bragg.

To my Families First, Inc. family, Vicki, Kristy, Greta, Jennifer, Ashley, Natasha, Rhonda, Lucy, Mary, Diane, Bertha Stephens, Janice, Ryan, John, Raven, Cheri, Kathy and all of their families.

I want to thank Families First, Inc. who has given me the opportunity to work with victims.

I want to thank all of my readers who read Pain No More 1, for their support and encouraging words.

Lastly, I would like to thank all of you who have been supportive of me throughout my life and who have always been there with an encouraging word, or a shoulder to lean on, you now who you are. I love you all dearly.

Introduction
By
Eather Mitchell

P ain No More Tooo, is based on the life story of a very loving Christian lady known as Shug. Shug was sheltered during her childhood, therefore reserved from the everyday games and lies of relationships with boys. She in no way knew the ropes of game playing. She thought her life as a married woman would be based on the "fairy tales" she once saw on television.

In her first book, Pain No More, you read about how her relationship and marriage to her childhood sweetheart or should I say, Satan from the pits of **HELL**. When Shug was first married, her life was somewhat of a "fairy tale". However, it did not take long for Shug to realize that her "fairy tale" of a marriage was actually a horrific dilemma of a nightmare. Shug introduced her husband, Haman to you and shared just a tidbit of information with you as to her life of domestic violence. In reading her first book, I'm sure you all asked yourselves, how could this be real? How could someone live in this and live through it to share it with the world? I know you all said, if it were me, I would have killed him or I would have done this or that? But, in reality, you don't know what you would have done, unless you actually were a victim of domestic violence yourself.

If you thought you were reading a horror story in her first book, Pain No More, just wait until you read, Pain No More Tooo. It will literally blow your mind. Shug is a survivor in every sense of the word. Today she carries a strong message to both men and women alike on the importance of a healthy relationship and the red flags of an unhealthy relationship. Shug is a **S-U-R-V-I-V-O-R!!!**

Chapter 1

Another New Start?

We left off talking about the new house. Shug wants you to know that the house is beautiful, located in a safe and family oriented neighborhood. She didn't have a white picked fence, but she had a back yard out of this world, with a built in grill. Now, Shug just knew that she had it all, until Haman came home and took his fist and punched Shug in the face. Then Shug looked at him with her hand covering her face with tears running down her face. Shug looked at Haman and asked him what was wrong? He never answered her. Haman was only interested in having his food on the table when he arrived home. After Haman ate his dinner, he would spend time asking the children about their day, never asking Shug about her day. As the evening grew, the children continued watching television. Shug would let them know that it was time to get ready for bed, realizing tomorrow is a school day. Their response would be, ok mommy. Now, they began to sound like something from Leave It To Beaver, ok honey. For Shug, this would make her night, at least for that moment. She thought to herself, so far so good. Shug would say, maybe this is going to be a good night. At the very moment when she was ready for bed, here comes the storm. After Haman would have his drink or drinks, he would have that look in his eyes. Well, you know at that moment Shug would experience the slap of a lifetime. After he slapped her, he began speaking Vietnamese. He would throw her on the bed and begin to have sex with her. As he was doing his business, Shug would look up at the ceiling and count. The next morning she would get the children ready for school. Haman has already left for work. The house was quiet; she would sit and have her morning coffee with sore swollen lips, crying, and wondering why, but could never come up with an answer. Every morning as Shug sipped on her coffee, her friend Peggy knocked at the door, just like clock work. Peggy would ask her, girl, where is my cup? I need my coffee too. As Peggy began to put sugar in her coffee, she noticed that Shug was not talking. Then as Shug turned around she saw Shug's face. Astoundingly, Peggy asked her, what in the world happen to you? Oh no honey, not again. Shug would tell her, oh it's alright. I just opened the closet door too quick and hit myself. She would say, yeah right. As the ladies would sip on their coffee, Shug would say something funny to make Peggy laugh, to get her to change the subject.

Then Peggy began to tell one of her stories by saying, now let me tell you something about Peggy. She was a mother of three, two sons and a daughter. Shug would always wonder if she was also in and abusive marriage just as she was. Shug never saw any bruises so she would say I guess not. The reason Shug wondered and wanted to know, because Peggy and her husband was not the best of married couples. She would tell Shug that she wanted a divorce, and now Shug wanted to know why, so Shug asked. Peggy, what in the world would make you want to get a divorce? Your husband seems to be a good husband and father. Peggy said to Shug, now honey, never judge a book by its cover. Peggy's husband would be out playing with their children, and they looked as if they were having so much fun. Looking back now, Shug would never see Peggy outside with them. Shug noticed the time and told Peggy, honey drink up fast. Shug would say, girl, I have to get this house clean and get dinner ready, and you know how that no good Haman is.

Later that afternoon, the children came home from school, and Shug wanted to have some fun with them, so they would go out into the backyard and have fun. Shug wanted to do something with them, before Haman would get home. Once Shug and the children finished playing in the yard, the children wanted to go and play with their friends, which was fine with Shug. Shug heard a car pulling up, and she heard M'Chella say, hi daddy. Shug froze right in her tracks and said, oh, here come the monster. Haman comes in the door and says, my darling Shug it's going to be a good night. Let me tell you something honey, it was.

Chapter 2

The Woman with the Stupid Smile

Haman woke up that morning wanting his coffee as usual. Shug asked him if he had a good night's sleep? He replied, yes, I did. What about you? Shug looked at him and said to herself, is this man really crazy or what? Honey, let me tell you something. I guess he forgot the night before he used Shug as a punching bag. Get this sugar lambs, he looked at Shug, and asked, what happen to you? Her face was all swollen with both eyes blacken. He had the nerve to ask her again, where have you have been to get that? He said well, I'm going to the unemployment office, and I'll be back soon. Shug was saying to herself don't ever come back, you monster. Shug started cleaning the house and getting up all the glass Haman broke the night before. Amazed at all the damage, all Shug could do was cry. I don't mean a soft cry, hard relentless crying. Honey, you know what I mean, a cry from the pit of your stomach. Get it together she said to herself, you never know when that monster will be walking back through the door. Hours pasted, and finally, it was quiet. All of a sudden, the door opened. Shug hears this stupid laugh. But, it was not Haman's laugh. It was more horrific than Haman's stupid laugh. Shug came out of the bedroom and Haman asked, guess who's coming for lunch? Haman brought this woman to the house, and all she could do was look at Shug and laugh, saying, oh you must be his sister? Now honey child, I guess you can image the look on Shug's face. Shug stood there looking at the woman saying to herself, is this a joke or a dream? No honey, it's not a dream or a joke. Haman told the woman this is my wife. The woman said, oh man, I know you said that earlier, I thought you were kidding me. Shug didn't think it was funny at all. Haman said, Shug, this is Lottie. I met her at the unemployment office, and we started talking. She was saying that she didn't like where she lived, so I asked her to come over and maybe we could help her. Now, up to this point, she still has not really introduced herself to Shug. Haman told Shug to make some lunch and turned to Lottie and asked her if she could use something to eat? Of course, yeah, why not she said? Shug watched the woman, as Haman gave her a tour of the house. I like this she said to Shug. This is nice with that big stupid smile. I live with my boyfriend and his mother. Girl, you know what I mean she said to Shug. Shug could care less where she lived. The only thing Shug knew was that this woman was in her house looking around as if it was open house or something. Was this woman one of Haman's next adventure or what? Now, Haman went out of his way to make sure that this woman with the dumbest look on her face she had ever seen knew where he lived.

Now Shug might have been dumb for letting Haman abuse her, but she has traveled down that road before.

After several weeks passed, Lottie came over and said girl, guess what? I'm getting married, as if Shug really cared. Shug said to herself, she is talking to me as if we were friends. Now honey let me tell you something, sit back and get ready, she had the nerve to ask Shug will you help me plan my wedding. Now you could imagine what was going on in Shug's head, is woman crazy or what? Shug would remember what her mother said, help someone no matter what. Can you believe Shug helped this woman? She was the same even when she got married, if you know what I mean.

Chapter 3

Nuclear Plant

Haman was still working at a nuclear plant in North Carolina. Haman met this woman at work and assumed they could car pool. Haman would tell Shug just in case you need the car today, I have to meet my woman at the plant. Haman was tired of his woman driving alone everyday. Haman thought it would be good if Shug would take the children somewhere or in case if there is an emergency the car would be here for me. Haman would always come home upset about something, this was his cue card. Every time this woman would come to pick Haman up, she would look at Shug as if to say, I got your man with that dumb smirk on her face.

As time went by, Haman and this woman got to know each other really well, and I mean "really well." To take the guilt off of him, Haman would come home upset, ready to start an argument with Shug. The name calling and beatings grew worst. Now all of a sudden Haman came home and said, he was going to move in with his woman and her sons. With everything Shug went through, now this. In a way Shug was hurt, but also elated of the fact, there would be no more abuse. On Saturday, the eve of Easter, Haman called Shug to tell her he was coming over to talk with her. Shug asked, what do you want to talk about? I'll tell you when I get there said Haman. Shug told M'Chella and Jack their daddy was coming over. M'Chella was happy, but Jack, on the other hand was not. When Haman knocked on the door, M'Chella raced to open the door and was so happy to see her daddy. Immediately after he entered the house, Haman said Shug, I need some money. Shug said, we don't have anything to eat in the house and we definitely don't have any money. Haman said, what you mean, no food and what am I suppose to do about that? Haman, you haven't given me any money for the children or anything. Well, I will give you something next week. Anyone who knows Shug, knows she has a kind heart and would do anything she could to help anyone. Shug went to the store and got some food for both her children as well as the woman's children. Unable to buy for her children, Shug bought Easter baskets for the woman's children. Even though Shug really didn't have anything at all for her children at the time, she never wanted to see any children go hungry. Jack, Shug's son was so upset, he told Shug that she was stupid to give daddy money and we don't have anything. Shug tried to explain to her son, you never let anyone go hungry no matter what they have done to you, and don't you ever call your mother stupid again. A friend of Shug came over to the house and asked her to go with her to the store, because she had to do some shopping for her children. Shug told her that she didn't have any money for shopping at this time. Alright, said her friend.

Once they got to the store, her friend put some things in the shopping cart for her children and Shug's too. They left that store and went to anther store, where they purchased some clothes for Shug's children. Shug was so happy she didn't know what to say or do. Shug's friend said, remember when I needed a friend you were there for me, and now I'm here for you. Shug just cried and gave her a big hug. Shug could not wait to get home to show her children what gifts they had. Shug wanted this to be a lesson to her son. She said you see son, you never know what God has in store for you when you help someone from the goodness of your heart without looking for something in return.

One day, Shug looked up and there stood Haman with his bags. He said, I'm back me and that woman could not get along anymore, but life was good for a few months. Haman was still working at the plant.

I often wondered if Haman treated his other woman as he treated me. Some days I was abused just as much emotionally as I was physically. Haman came home from work this one particular evening and said to Shug, my friend said when you give me a divorce she will be ready to have sex with me, but honey, not in that manner.

Now, when Shug heard this, she said to herself, alright that's good, again she dared to say that aloud. Shug would go back and forth to the door and watch the children play, while Haman cleaned up for dinner. It was a nice day, sunny and bright. Shug would often wonder, what in the world had I done to deserve this punishment from someone who was suppose to love and protect her?

Shug had something else on her mind. So she contacted Shanté a good friend of hers from New Jersey. She helped her when she left Haman in New Jersey. Shanté asked, what is going on Shug? Shug told her to get over to her house as soon as she could. When Shanté arrived, Shug explained to her what Haman told her the woman from his job said. Shanté said, I know you're kidding right? Shug said, does it look like I'm kidding? Shanté asked, what are you going to do? Well honey, this is where you come in. I want you to drive me to the Nuclear Plant. What! said Shanté? Yes, I'm going to see who this woman is. This is the woman Haman argues and beat me over, and it's time to see this slut. Shug made arrangements with the neighbor to watch her children, M'Chella and Jack until she got back. As they drove up to the plant, Shanté was so amazed with Shug. I just can't believe you are going up there. What are you going to do when you get there? Shug said, now look honey, you are asking two many questions. I have an hour and a half to figure it out. Well, here we are Shanté said; now what? Shug told her to drive her up to the gate and park the car. Shug got out of the car and walked toward the security guard. All the time, she was looking around hoping to see Haman. The security guard asked, how can I help you? She replied. I'm here to see my husband. The security guard said unless you are an employee, you can't go into the gate. All of a sudden Shug heard a voice, it was that no good Haman. Shug hurriedly walked pass the guard and went to where Haman was. Now you have to know Shug. She was always dressed to kill, and looking good. Some of the men sitting with Haman looked at Shug, and wondered who was this good looking woman walking toward them? Yeah, I said good looking in every since of the word. Haman looked up and saw me and turned around. He knew I was not the dog he was looking to have sex with. Finally, all of his friends and co-workers got to see this woman for what she was. Haman walked up to Shug and asked, what are you doing here? Shug said, I came to see the slut that told you to tell me if I give you a divorce she will have sex with you. So Shug saw this big Amazon woman sitting quietly on a stump. She turned and looked at Shug and said, oh, you must be the one. At this point, Shug literally lost her mind. She asked Haman to give her the car keys and he said no. Shug asked him a second time, give me the keys. Finally, Haman gave her the keys. Then he had the nerve to ask Shug, are you coming back to pick me up? Shug turned around and said, stay with your slut or have her to bring your no good behind home. As Shug walked away, she had a sigh with relief saying, what is going to happen when he gets home? In the mean while, Shug had the upper hand for once, which that made her feel real gooooooooooooood.

When Haman arrived home that night, you can imagine what had happened. He started yelling, telling Shug, you embarrassed me in front of my friends. Shug said, and don't forget your slut too. Shug dared Haman to touch her in any way if you know what I mean. Do you think Shug is going to do anything while Haman is asleep? Alright honey, what would you do? Keep that to yourself. Before he went to work, he called his friend Lottie. At this point, Shug really could care less what he called her for. Lottie came over and wanted to talk to Shug. Shug opened the door, and Lottie walked in. Shug gave her the meanest look anyone had ever seen. Meanwhile, Haman was in the room, when he heard Lottie's voice he came out of the room to make himself known.

Shug just walked away with a big smile on her face.

Chapter 4

Greyhound 1980

In 1979, Shug decided that she wanted to do something different and better with her life, instead of constant abuse both verbally and physically. She spoke to Haman to get his input. Little did he know, she already made up her mind. Shug went to Raleigh NC to apply for a Greyhound bus driver position. Months went by without hearing from the company. Shug began to get a little worried because she knew she met all of the requirements to become a driver. Meanwhile, as Shug was waiting she still was going through the abuse. One day the telephone rang, and the voice on the other end, asked for Shug. The person stated they were calling from the Greyhound Bus Station in Raleigh NC, and wanted to know if she could come in for an interview. Shug was so happy she just yelled out yes I certainly can, and I will be there and thank you, thank you very much. When Shug hung up the phone she was so happy that she forgot about that monster Haman. Oh my goodness, she said, what in the world will I tell him? Whatever it was it was alright because she was not going to worry about that now. She was too happy and excited. Shug said, I'm going to celebrate with a cup of coffee. Now let me tell you something honey, Shug just wanted to sit and take it all in. If you have ever been in a situation you like that, then you know exactly what Shug is trying to tell you. As the hours passed, the children came home from school, and Shug was so happy to see them, she wanted to tell them the news. Do you think she told them? Oh no! She had to wait until Haman got home, which was a couple of hours later. Now Shug made a special meal, something she knew would make Haman happy. Oh no, I know what you are thinking it wasn't Chitterlings. It was fried chicken. She had the table all set when Haman walked through the door. Hello Haman, how was your day? You know why she asked. She had to know whether to tell him of her good news now or to keep it a secret little longer, even though she was about to burst. Haman said, it was ok and why do you ask? Although Shug would ask him that everyday, he felt there was something different about this time. She said, oh nothing. Haman talked to Jack and M'Chella, before dinner to see what he could find out. Shug was watching Haman all the time, and asking herself should I tell him or not? Not yet, she said to herself.

Well, now is the time, Shug said to herself. She decided to have Jack and M'Chella present. Shug felt with them present maybe Haman would not act a fool. Shug asked Haman if he wanted anything else, and he replied no. Haman, a few months ago, I put in an application for Greyhound Bus Lines, and received one of the positions. I will leave for

Jacksonville, Florida in two weeks. I will be there for four weeks. Now in Shug's mind that was a gigantic relief, no abuse, no name calling, no fighting. Well, Haman said, when are you leaving? What happens with Jack and M'Chella? I told him they will be fine. I have already made arrangements. After school they will be staying with friends, and when you get home from work, the children will come home. Shug said to Haman, you are off on the weekend, so you can take care of them, and everything will be fine. Shug told the kids that she will be talking to them every night, and with me getting this job and going to this school, I will be able to get a better job. I will be sending money home every week for anything that you should need. Both of the children said ok mommy, we love you. Shug said, I love you too very much. Although it was painful, she realized, she will be leaving her children, but it's not for selfish reasons or was it? Maybe a selfish reason would come into play just to get away from Haman, and his abuse. In her mind, all she could see was a better future for her and her children.

Haman wanted to be close with Shug the night before she was to leave. She really had no desire to be with him, but she knew if she didn't, he would beat her and she would be leaving with bruises all over her. Against her desire of him touching her, she did what he wanted. Now was it ok, not at all. As they became close she caught herself counting. Yes, honey counting, until it was all over.

Shug began saying, it's here. I am on my way to a new career. Oh, by the way, you know Shug had a P.H.D. in hard Knocks, if you know what I'm saying. Haman drove her to the station along with her children. It was very sad in a way, and glad in another. The sad was leaving her children, but she knew she had to do something if she was to have a better life for her and the children. Glad, oh yes! No more Haman calling her names and beating her for weeks at a time. Door one for Jacksonville, Florida shouted the bus driver. She gave her children a big hug and kiss, and she told them how much she loved them. Now, as for Haman she just gave him a simple hug, and a peck on his lips.

Once she was on the bus, she began to rub off her lips. Shug boarded the bus with tears in her eyes, but she knew her children would be alright.

Shug arrived in Jacksonville for her training, and met some interesting people. She had a wonderful room mate. Shug's roommate had children also. They had a lot in common. She didn't want to leave her children either, which she was looking for the same thing as Shug, a better career. Shug would call her children every night, and you know she would end the call telling them she loved them. Once she hung up the phone, she would be so sad, and the tears began to flow. Now it was hard at first for Shug, but she managed. Now let me tell you what her salary was each week. Brace yourself and remember this was in 1980. Her weekly check was $125.00. She would send home $100.00 and she would keep $25.00 for herself to eat or whatever. Shug would have to live off of $100.00 for the month, ok honey. I know what you are thinking, what in the world?

Well, Shug has been in Jacksonville for four weeks, it was time to go home. Shug had a big smile and couldn't wait to see her children. Shug would also miss her friends she met there, but she will see them again. As the bus pulled into the terminal, she looked out of the window and saw her children standing there, oh yea and so was Haman.

Shug jumped off the bus and gave Jack and M'Chella a big hug and kiss and just said hello to Haman. Shug got some gifts for the children, and could not wait until they got home. Later that night, guess what

Haman wanted. Oh my goodness Shug said, I'm so tired from the trip, let's do this tomorrow. Of course you know Haman was back to his old self, you must have had someone in Florida. Shug asked Haman, why would you say something like that? I'm just tired Shug kept saying. You know why Shug wanted to go to sleep, oh you know why.

Chapter 5

Christmas Eve 1980

It was Christmas Eve, and Shug was excited. She knew her children would have a good Christmas since she has been working. Thanksgiving and Christmas were her best holidays. Growing up, Shug would recall her parents going all out for Christmas. Shug would always remember what her mother told her, it was better to give than to receive. Well, this Christmas Eve is one night she would never forget not ever. Haman was in the bedroom when all of a sudden the door bell rang. Now, Shug, all happy and excited she answered the door, and there stood a woman just as tall as Haman. Shug answered the door saying, hello and Merry Christmas. When Shug opened the door, this woman pushed her way into door and demanded to see Haman. Now honey, what do you think Shug said? What would you say? This lady said, you heard me" B". I came for Haman. Now here comes this fool from the bedroom with his kit. Let's go back a bit. Remember, in Jersey, Haman went to school for cosmetology. Shug asked Haman, where are you going? Instead of him answering, this woman answered the question for him; he's going with me. What! With you, said Shug. That's what I said. Now, Haman was listening to all of this and told Shug, I'm going to do her family's hair for the holidays. Shug looked at him and asked are you crazy? Meanwhile, this woman is telling Haman to come on, we have to get to Sanford we have people waiting for us. Shug said now wait a minute, its Christmas Eve Haman you need to be here for the children when they wake up. What are you going to do, Shug asked? I will be back before they get up, said Haman. Haman walked out the door with this woman, and Shug could not and didn't know how to take this. Shug called one of her friends to come and watch the children for her. Now Shug has been beat up, called some of the ugliest names, and now this. She said, oh no, I don't think so. Shug at this point snapped. She went into the kitchen and got five steak knives. She followed them to the gas station, and yes honey there they were getting gas. Shug got out of her car and told Haman that he needed to come back to the house and be there when the children got up the following morning. She reminded him, he could at least do that, since you haven't been a good father to them in the past. Haman said no, I will be back later. Shug said that was not good enough. I believe she had a flashback of what Haman did to her in the past. Shug pulled out one of the knives, and flipped it and just missed Haman's arm. Shug kept flipping the knives until she got to her last one, at this time a policeman was called to the scene. To Shugs surprise, she knew him. He asked her, what are you doing? As I said earlier Shug snapped. She asked him, what does it look like to you? He told her he had to take her to jail. She said ok, but I have one more knife to go. Since I'm going to jail, I need to throw this one. She did and that one just missed Haman's head. Shug was placed in the police car, and the police told Haman to ride in front, because he had to go to the police station also.

Shug had to face the magistrate, and let me tell you something, Shug was scared. After the police officer took her inside the office, she was still in hand cuffs. This man sitting behind the desk was so familiar to Shug. He asked, don't I know you from somewhere? Shug took another look at him while she was trying to see if she knew him. While reminding Shug where he remembered her, on the other hand, Shug was saying to herself, I sure hope he does. He asked, didn't you work at the gas station on Reilly Road? Shug replied, well, yes, I still do. Now, Shug is still standing there with handcuffs on and they were behind her back. The Magistrate asked the police officer, what did this young lady do? The police officer laid in front of the Magistrate five steak knives. Your honor she was throwing them at her husband, said the police officer. Take those handcuffs off of her. You won't hurt me would you? Of course not, said Shug. As he officer removed the cuffs, Shug took a deep breath and said thank you to the officer. Will you please tell me why you were throwing these knives asked the Magistrate? Shug was getting ready to answer, when she was interrupted by the magistrate. Didn't you also drive buses or something? Shug said yes, I am a Greyhound bus driver now. Shug asked your honor is this Christmas candy, may I have a piece? Why yes, said the Magistrate. Now, please tell me what happened to cause you to go to this extreme. Shug told him this woman came to her door, asking for her husband, and as she was pushing her way into the door, she was calling Haman. He came out of the room, saying I'm going with her to do her families' hair. Shug told him this is Christmas Eve, and you need to be here. Now let me tell you something, as Haman was telling Shug he was leaving, this lady was telling Haman come on we have to go. My husband started walking out of the door with this woman. At this time, all I wanted to do was to hurt this man just as much as he hurt me. Shug asked the magistrate, what would you do, if a man came to your home and told you he was there to pick up your wife, and she was getting ready to go with him. Meanwhile, this man is calling you all kinds of names. Now the Magistrate asked, on or off the record? Shug said she didn't care which it was. He told her, I would try to hurt him also. Shug said that's what I was trying to do. That is why I'm standing here in front of you right now. The Magistrate said, I believe I could understand what you were going through, but you handled it the wrong way. Now with all that said and done, I'm going to talk to your husband and also that young lady. He called the woman in, and she had to walk right in front of Shug. Could you imagine what was on Shug's mind? Yes, tripping her, ok. Was she wrong for thinking that she's human? As the magistrate was talking to her, she had an attitude and a very nasty one at that. The magistrate asked her, did she live in Fayetteville? She said no, I live in Sanford. Why did you come to Fayetteville? She said, I came to get my friend Haman. I came to pick him up and take him home with me. Now, can you imagine what this girl must look like? This was a very disrespectful girl. Just listen to the way she talks. Did you know this man was married? Yea, she said. Now the magistrate told her she need to go back to Sanford and don't even think about coming back to Fayetteville. This woman asked the magistrate what about Haman? He told her that she needs to leave or he will put her in jail for contempt. The magistrate told the police to escort her to her car, and young lady you need you need to take my advise and don't be caught back here again. If you do, and you are reported, I will see that you be placed in jail. So that was the end of her for that night. Now on the other hand, Haman had to speak with the Magistrate. He told

Haman he was not to go to Sanford to see anyone that night. Shug had already told the Magistrate that she didn't want him to come home that night with all that had happened. Shug left and went home to be with the children for the rest of Christmas Eve.

The next day was Christmas day, and guess who was at the door, wanting to come in. Now honey, if it wasn't for the children Shug would have left him standing outside. Jack and McChella were glad to see Haman. They had no idea what had taken place the night before. Shug had to say it was a good and peaceful Christmas.

Chapter 6

Body Search

When you hear of the term "body search", what do you think of? Having to go through metal detectors at the airports, federal buildings, schools and some hospitals, kind of make me think of the term. Would you ever think that you would have a body search just for going to the grocery store or any store for that matter? Shug would like to take you back just a little.

In the past, Shug went through some embarrassing things, being beaten in front of friends, yelled at in the stores, and called everything other than her name. But she never thought she would have to go through what you are about to read. Now Haman was not only an abuser, he was also an obsessively jealous man. You read in the past about Haman's behavior. No matter what Shug would do he would put her down, trying to break her self-esteem down so low where she would not care for anyone or herself. He also kept tabs on her. What's wrong with this picture? Even though Shug would never let him know he was wearing her down, several times all she wanted to do was to give up. During the blistering summer heat where the temperature would be one hundred degrees or more, Shug would walk around wearing a turtleneck sweater, just so no one could see the bruises on her neck. Shug looked at other women, and wondered if they were going through the same thing as she was. She often wondered if it was common for them to be beaten and called names. Shug could only wonder, do other women have to have sex with their husband or mate, even when they desire not to? Watching them when she frequented places, she would just look and wonder, when they got home what are they facing, a slap, punch or terrible name calling? Does their companion respect them, or do they tear them down with every kind of abuse there was? Can you imagine what is going on in Shug's head, one can only imagine.

This one particular day, Haman came home from work in a good mood. Shug was stunned. Shug wanted to ask him why was he so happy, but you know Shug, you better not ask Haman that question. Matter of fact, not only that question, but any question. Now that Haman was in a good mood, Shug wanted to know if Haman wanted to go to the store. Shug had some shopping to do, and she knew if she asked him any questions that would create another monster. Therefore, she thought it might be a little better on her that night. Well here goes. Shug called Haman's name and he turn around and looked at her as if to say, what in the world do you want. If looks could kill, Haman surely would have killed Shug that night. Shug said, I need to go to the store, and pick up a few things from the store. Haman said ok, I'll take you, are you ready? Yes she replied. Just let me get the children. While going to the store, Haman said he was going out that night so make sure you get what ever you need because he would be gone for a few days. Now Shug wanted to ask where are you going, but to her it was all-good, at least she could get some rest. Haman was in a good mood even when he was at the store. Once they got home Haman received a phone call, and his mood changed. All of a sudden he wasn't happy anymore. Shug asked, what's wrong Haman? He just looked at her saying nothing. For the remainder of the night Haman was quiet until they went to bed. Haman told Shug, it's all your fault. If I hadn't taken you to the store, I would have been able to leave earlier, Haman was so upset he gave Shug a punch in her face and said good night "B". Haman left for work the next morning, he didn't wake Shug up to make coffee and he normally did. This was strange to Shug, because you see this was a Saturday and Haman never worked on Saturdays. Shug went to the bathroom and took a good look at the side of her face, and saw the damage Haman did to her once again. Maybe that's why he left, because he saw what he did to her. All Shug knew, he never left her at the house before so why now? Your guess is just as good as Shug's. Shug put on enough makeup so the children could not see her bruised face. That day Shug and the children had a fun day together. They cleaned their rooms perfectly. Then, Shug said, lets' make something together. McChella always wanted to know, what are we doing tonight? Let's make cookies or a cake which ever you want to. McChella said, I want to make both. Jack asked Shug if he could go play with some of his friends while you girls bake. Shug said ok, but his sister asked, why won't you eat anything I make? If you don't want to help us, go ahead son and play. It was a fun day for all. Haman came home and wanted to know what was for dinner? Shug said that slipped her mind, since her and McChella was having so much fun. But, I will have dinner ready in a few minutes

Shug replied. Now wherever Haman went he was not a happy camper when he came back home. Shug told Haman, I forgot something I need to get from the store. I'll be back shortly. Haman was upset about that. Why do you have to go to the store now? Who are you going to meet? Shug looked at him and said, what did you say? Haman repeated it again. Shug looked at him and wanted to say, why, would I want another man, but dared to say that. Shug went to the store. When she returned, she found an upset Haman because she didn't take McChella with her. Did you do meet your man, Haman asked? He took Shug in the bedroom and did a body search, and I mean a full body search all over. Haman checked her underwear if you know what I mean. He was not happy at all. What he fixated in his mind was not so. He slapped Shug and told her to hurry and put on dinner. After dinner, the family sat down and watched television together.

The next morning, Shug woke up to something smelling good in the kitchen. Haman and the children were cooking breakfast. Shug thought, you all sure know how to put a smile on Shug's face. Haman made plans for the entire day. He invited some friends over to watch the game on television, and began to make snacks and get things ready. Now, Shug was happy and felt this Sunday will be a good day. It was one o'clock and his company began to arrive. Shug never met them. They were some of his co-workers. Shug said hello to them all and asked, if she could get them anything? They replied, no thank you. Although Shug was expressing good ole' hospitality, Haman gave her a look as if to say, what are you doing? Haman was already drinking Vodka, so Shug excused herself and went into the bedroom. Jack and McChella were watching the game with their father. The game stayed on for a few hours. After the game went off, Haman's friends began to leave. Shug told them all good bye and thanked them for coming and hoped to see them again. That night Shug was confronted by Haman. He wanted to know why she thanked them for coming. That was all it took and it was on. Haman slapped Shug across her face. She looked at Haman and asked, what in the world is wrong with you? He said you must have liked one of my friends. I don't have to tell you what happen that night in the bedroom. Haman forced Shug to have sex with him as she was lay there crying. The next day was a work day for Haman, but he decided not to go to work that day. Shug got the children off to school, and asked Haman if he wanted some coffee. He replied, no "B". Haman told Shug to go to the store and get him something. Shug knew deep down inside something was getting ready to happen. Therefore, she asked everyone in line at the register if she could go ahead of them. They all looked at her and said yes. They all could tell something was not right and she was terrified. Once Shug got home Haman was waiting for her with his hands ready to attack. But little did he know, Shug knew the attack was not on her body, but checking her body. He accused Shug of having sex with someone while gone to the store. After checking and body searching her, he slapped her and said, I know you did something. It doesn't take twenty minutes to go to the store. This particular beating seemed as if it was an all day beating. Haman would stop before the children got home from school. By the time Haman stopped beating her, she looked as if she had been in a boxing match and lost with blood all over her. Shug cleaned herself up before the children came into the house. Once the children got home, Haman began to play with the children while Shug got dinner ready. That night Shug knew she would have to withstand another beating, without making a sound.

Chapter 7

Naptime, Before Work

Let me refresh your memory, Shug was a Greyhound bus driver. When Shug wasn't driving the bus, she would work as a cashier at the convenient store. Now, while working there, Shug would meet many interesting people, which helped make her day go by faster. When women came to get gas, they began to build a trusting relationship with Shug. They would tell her their problems and what they were experiencing with their mates. Although Shug was struggling, she would say to them, it will get better if you just hang in there. Now the women who were talking to her didn't know that Shug was going through similar problems. Shug would never see any physical scares on them, or they were hiding them just as she was. Shug's customers would come into the store and pay for their gas and Shug's day by saying something good which would put a smile on Shug's face. When time came for Shug to go home, she couldn't wait to get there to see Jack and McChella the love of her life. Now being the mother of two beautiful children with an abusive husband, she realized all her joy came from her children. As Shug prepared dinner, she would just look at them playing and having fun with each other. That alone would put a smile on her face.

Shug looked at the clock and thought to herself, what would take place in a few hours. She pondered and asked herself, would it be a good night or a horrific night? Shug was in the kitchen and all of a sudden, she heard a car pulling into the garage. The children turned around and looked at Shug wondering what will Haman do when he come through the door. As the key turned to unlock the door, the children began to panic. When the door opened, in comes this man with the smell of booze. What's for dinner, he asked. He refused to ask Shug how her day was. He went over and talk to the children. The children asked Shug if they could go outside. She said, just for a few minutes dinner will be ready shortly. Shug and Haman were alone in the house together at this time. Some women would think that is a good thing, but to Shug it was not pleasant at all. He would come into the kitchen and look into the pots to see what was cooking. Shug asked him, how was your day? It was good, he said. Shug called the children in for dinner. She was scared to ask Haman anything else. After dinner the children watched television before getting ready for bed. Shug cleaned the kitchen and got ready for bed herself. As she walked to her bedroom, she said, I hope he's asleep when I get in there. Although, the bedroom was only a few steps, it felt like I was walking a mile. As she got to the door, she saw Haman sleeping. Thank goodness, it's going to be a good night after all. Shug was very careful not to wake him as she climbed into the bed.

During the night, Shug was awakened by Haman's hands going across her body, and believe me, they were not welcomed. Haman wanted to have sex, something Shug didn't want to have at all with this man. He wanted to kiss her and all she could do was hold her breathe. Haman's breathe was disgusting, she would turn her face, knowing that would make Haman mad, but she didn't care. He climbed on top of her to do his business. As he began, she would look up to the ceiling and count, and then it was all over as quickly as it started. Although, Shug knew she had to perform her wifely duties, she always felt nasty and dirty afterwards. She would jump up immediately and clean herself up.

Shug would lay there wondering if other women were going through the same thing at night. Shug would always get up a few hours before her day would start and wash clothes and get the children's clothes ready for school. Shug prepared Haman's lunch then she enjoyed a little quiet time to herself. Suddenly, the alarm clock goes off, she heard Haman getting up. While he was getting ready for work, Shug made his coffee. Haman came into the kitchen and said, good morning and that would be all he said.

As he gathered his work gear, Shug would go into the bedroom waiting for him to leave. When she heard the door close a big smile would come over her face. Yes, the monster is gone. Shug would lay down for a couple of hours until it was time to get the children up for school. After getting the children off to school, Shug began cleaning the house and getting dinner ready. She had to go to work that afternoon. When Shug finished her house hold chores, she laid down to take a nap before going to work. Haman brought one of his friends from work to the house that afternoon. Haman called for Shug but got no answer. He walked down the hall into the bedroom and saw that Shug was sleeping, so he turned around and walked out of the bedroom back into the living room where his friend was. After talking and drinking with his friend for awhile, Haman went back into the bedroom where Shug was. But, instead of him calling her name, he took a ceramic lamp and busted it in the back of Shug's head. Shug woke up with blood all over the bed. Shug asked Haman, what was wrong with him? He started beating Shug, while his friend was in the living room. Again, Shug had no one to help her. Shug got up and cleaned the blood off the back of her head. She felt dizzy as if she was going to faint. But, she knew that she had to go to work. Shug walked by the living room and saw Haman's friend sitting there. He turned around and looked at Shug, not saying a word to her. I guess he was afraid to say anything because he did not know exactly what kind of man Haman was.

Shug went to work feeling dizzy and sore. Every time Shug would ring up someone's order and looked down to put money in the cash register or get change, her nose would start bleeding. Her customers would ask her is she was alright. Shug would always say yes, knowing that she wasn't. Shug worked like that for six hours, until her shift ended. As the night went by, Shug started getting sick to her stomach. Shug would wonder what in the world got into Haman. Why would he do something like that to me? I don't know why she would say to herself. She didn't know what kind of man Haman was. A customer came into the store and saw Shug crying, and asked her, what was wrong? She said nothing. But, when she went to get the customer's change, her nose started bleeding again. He asked her again, what's wrong with you? This time Shug tells him. He suggested she go to the hospital and get checked. He said you might have a concussion. Shug said, thank you very much for your concern. Well, the time had come for shug to go home. What do you think she did? Did Shug go to the hospital or straight home? You got it sugarlamb, she went straight home. She was afraid Haman would wonder where she was. I wonder what was on Shug's mind when she got home. Would she tell Haman she wanted to go to the hospital or would she just take care of herself the best way she could. No, she didn't go to the hospital. When she got home, there was Haman sitting there wondering what took her so long to get home. She was home in ten minutes once she left her job.

Haman still refused to ask her how she was doing, or say he was sorry. He would just look at her. Shug looked in on the children while they were sleeping, making sure they were alright. Shug asked Haman if the children had eaten dinner. He said, what you think? Shug waited until Haman went to sleep to take a bath and take care of her bruises. Now, believe me when I tell you she was very sore, but she knew she would be alright once she got a good night's sleep.

Chapter 8

Being Accused

Shug went to work early this day, therefore, she was able to go home and get dinner ready, and help the children with their homework. Once Jack and McChella finished their homework, Shug went outside to play with them for awhile. Then they asked Shug if they could go and play with their friends before dinner, or before daddy comes home. Shug said yes, just for a little while. Shug heard Haman pulling into the car port. She hurried to set the table before Haman opened the door. Shug said hello Haman, how was your day? Haman put his work gear down, and slapped Shug across the face. He threw the food on the floor, even the food that was still in the pots. He threw everything all over the floor. Shug asked, Haman what in the world is wrong with you? The children heard the loud noise and came running. Haman told them everything was alright, go back and play. Once the children left, Haman began beating Shug just as if she was a man. Blood splattered all over the place. Haman threw Shug over the table onto the floor. He pulled her by her hair, and punched her in her face. By this time, Shug was out of it, but still breathing. She recalled seeing Haman walking down the hall, but she just could not get the strength to get up. Haman returned and starting beating Shug again. At this point, all Shug could do was plead with him to please stop. Haman helped her to her feet, telling her to clean herself up and fix him some food. But, she had no food left in the pots. Haman threw everything on the floor. Shug went into the bathroom and started to clean herself up. She made the mistake and looked in the mirror, and what she saw was nothing short of a monster. She did the best she could so the children would not see all of her bruises. She hurried to find and fix Haman something to eat. Haman noticed the children were coming into the house, so he told them to stay outside for a few more minutes. Your mother is cleaning up the floor. Shug got something together. Oh yeah, guess what. She gave him some of the food that was on the floor without Haman knowing it. Shug thought and hoped that maybe some of her blood might have fallen in the plate also. That serves him right, she thought to herself. The children came into the house and washed their hands for dinner. Jack looked and said, mommy what happen to the food and looking at Haman at the same time. He knew Haman done something to his mommy. The children sat down with Haman to eat their dinner while Shug went into the bedroom. Once the children finished, Shug told them to take their baths and get ready for bed, but they could watch television only a few minutes.

Shug waited until Haman was finished with his food, then she sat down and ask him, why did he beat her like an animal? She wanted to know what had she done for that kind of treatment? He said, his friend at work told him earlier he saw me out at the club. Shug looked at him and asked did you believe him? He said, he has no reason to lie to me. Shug said may I ask you something, he said yeah "B". Shug said last night was Thursday right, he said yeah "B". Shug said, don't you remember we watched Thursday Night at the Movies? Haman said yeah, so what. Shug asked, what did we watch after the movie went off? He said what? Shug said, we watched the eleven o'clock news. Again he said so what. Shug said after that then what did we do? He said you know we had sex, but not in those words. Shug looked up at him and asked, when did I leave the house? All he could say was oh well. That sorry piece of a man would not even tell Shug that he was sorry. Haman got up from the table and went into the living room where the children were. Shug waited a few minutes then she told Jack and McChella to tell their daddy good night. Later, Shug went in and gave them a kiss good night. When she went into Jack's room he asked Shug, are you alright mommy? Shug said, yes, baby I am. Don't you worry just get a good night's sleep. Shug returned to the kitchen and began cleaning the kitchen. As she was cleaning, she notice blood was still all over the kitchen. She even found a piece of her flesh on the wall. The kitchen was a mess, food all over the walls, counters tops and floor. While she was cleaning, she was wondering, what could she do to this man? She wondered if she could kill him while he sleeps or should she just poison him. Shug just shook her head and said to herself, what would happen to my Jack and McChella if I go to jail. By this time, Shug's mother and father were deceased and she didn't have any siblings. That thought quickly left her head. After cleaning the kitchen, Shug got the children's school clothes ready for the next day. Shug was afraid to go to bed, wondering if he was asleep or not. She wondered, what would he do to her or what kind of act he wanted her to perform on him? Shug took a long hot bath to relax her banged up body. Shug was getting tired so she decided to go to bed. Yes honey. Haman was sleeping with entire room smelling like liquor. Shug had some bad thoughts roaming through her mind. If I killed him now, what would happen to me, or what in the world would happen to my children? All I would have to do is hit him in the head with a hammer or something. Shug had to shake it off. She couldn't do that not just yet. Shug would ease into the bed hoping not to wake Haman, and she was successful. Shug would toss and turn all night long, and her body ached with pain. Shug slept with one eye open and the other closed, if you know what I mean.

Chapter 9

Cheerleader Coach

Shug had a friend that lived in this housing area, who offered after school activities for her children, such as a variety of sports according to the season. They also offered cheerleading for the girls. Shug was so interested, she made some phone calls the following day, trying to find out how and what she needed to do to get Jack and McChella enrolled. She talked it over with the children to see if they wanted to participate in the activities. Of course, Jack said. Do they have football mama? Shug looked at Jack and yes, baseball too. McChella said, what about me? Shug said yes, they have activities for you also. Shug signed Jack up for football. Oh, that made Shug so happy, that her friend told her about this program. She knew this would keep the children occupied and happy in the mist. When

Shug took the children to the field the next day, she met some of the other mothers. Again, she looked at them and wondered if they were going through the same or similar things she was going through. She wondered if they were in an abusive relationship. Although she wondered these things, she was just happy she was able to meet and mingle with other women her age. As the mothers sat and watched the boys practice, they began to wonder, why there were no cheerleaders practicing. One of the mothers got the coach's attention and asked him, where are the cheerleaders? He said they didn't have a coach for the cheerleaders. It would be good, if we could find a coach for the cheerleaders. As the mothers sat there looking at each other, they wondered, who can we get? Shug just sat there, without uttering a word. We all looked at each other, and all our voices rang out saying, well not me. So they all looked at Shug at the same time. Shug looked at McChella wanting her to do something also. So, Shug agreed and said she would be their coach. Now, let me tell you something honey, Shug didn't know the first thing about being a cheerleader coach. But, she was going to give it a try. All the mothers agreed, they would give Shug a hand whenever she needed it. Shug is now talking to herself saying, what have I gotten myself into? Well, on the way home, she tells McChella she is going to be their cheerleader coach. Jack said what, you are going to be what mama? Shug said yes, is something wrong with that honey? Jack just looked at Shug shaking his head. Now, Shug is wondering what in the world is she going to tell that Haman, that evil husband of hers? After getting the children home, Shug hurried to prepare dinner hoping Haman would not get upset when he came through the door. The children met Haman outside, and yes, they told Haman about Shug being the cheerleader's coach. When Haman walked into the house he looked at Shug and kept walking toward the bathroom. Imagine you in Shug's shoes wondering if Haman was coming out of the room angry or not. Haman came and sat down at the kitchen table. He asked, what is this the children are telling me about you being the cheerleaders coach? Shug said, why yes. They need a coach and I volunteered. Haman asked, when are you going to have the time to do that? Shug said, I have to make time, this is for McChella, and she wasn't involved in anything, so I thought she can be a cheerleader for Jack's team at the games. Haman just looked at Shug, and if looks could kill she would be dead.

That evening, Shug was walking on eggs shells wondering what was on Haman's mind. Shug couldn't stop thinking about being a cheerleader coach. Oh man, this is really going to be fun she thought, laughing on the inside. Shug looked up and Haman came walking toward her with this look in his eyes, as if he wanted to slap her. But to Shug's surprise, he told her since you are doing this for McChella it was alright. Shug looked at Haman and said thank you. Now that's sad when you have to get permission from a man to do things for your children or for yourself. But you see honey, Shug had to get permission from a man who has done nothing but abuse her. The next day, Shug took Jack to practice and noticed that the mothers brought some more girls there. Shug asked the mothers, what was going on? They said, you needed some girls so here they are. Shug said, oh well, lets get started. Shug starting taking the girls name, addresses and phone numbers. Shug was so excited. Shug asked the mothers if they could help with getting the girls uniforms together.

After practice Shug had to go to work at the gas station, and get dinner ready before Haman came home. McChella was so excited she couldn't wait until practice the next day. All she could talk about with Jack was, I'm going to be a cheerleader. Shug went to work wondering how she was going to do this. She wondered, if she was going to have Haman's support or was he going to continue with his abuse. Later that night when Shug got home Haman was still up waiting for her. Shug said hello Haman, how was your day? He looked at her and said fine, and how was your day? Shug was so excited she told him the other mothers brought some girls to the field to become cheerleaders. Isn't that's great? All Haman said was, I guess. Shug asked Haman, did you enjoy your dinner? Yes why? Shug was wondering if this is going to be a good night or is Haman going to start acting like a fool. Shug stayed up writing the girls names on index cards with their information. Shug, get in this bed right now, Haman yell out. Shug said to herself, he don't sound too good. Once shug got in the bedroom Haman said, you need to come to bed, and you all know what that meant. As Shug got ready for bed Haman just looked at her. Once she got into bed Haman wanted to do his business. But, Shug was not on the same page with Haman. Shug realized that Haman knew something was wrong. He just slapped Shug and told her she needed to get her head together and you know what that meant. Haman said, if you don't do it right you know what you are going to get. That night Shug took a couple of knocks and woke up the next morning with some more bruises.

The next day Shug was sore all over, but she could not let that stop her. When she arrived at the ball field and saw all of the girls excited and ready for practice, Shug had to put all of her hurt on the back burner. Shug had the girls do some warm up exercises to get started. Now, remember, Shug had to do angel splits with the girls also. Now, can you image Shug bruised and sore all over how she must have felt? But, the show must go on, Shug said. When Shug noticed how excited the girls were she couldn't think of anything else but to keep them that way. They would yell to their mothers saying, mom look at me. The mothers would yell back, yes we see you. After practice the mothers came over and thanked Shug for doing this for the team. The other mothers had no idea, that, Shug's entire body was sore and bruised by the hands of her own husband. Shug knew how important it was for the girls and the other mothers that she kept them happy and cheering. So with that big contagious smile of hers, that is just what she did.

Chapter 10

Moving Again

Well, Haman and Shug have been renting their home for sometime now. They were under the impression they would be in line to purchase the home. But, later they found out the home was in foreclosure, and the purchase price was far too much for them to handle at the time.

In a way, Shug was happy to move. She felt this house was not a home. It reminded her of all the beatings she had to take. If only walls could talk. I believe they would have told you a story that was utterly unbelievable. Come to think about it, if Shug wasn't married to Haman, Shug would have tried to purchase it for her and the children. They were looking for a house where their children would attend school in the same district and not have to change schools. Surprisingly, they were able to find a nice house in the same district. Moving and working as a bus driver was very hard. Someone had to do it. Haman would help sometimes when he wasn't drunk. Otherwise, the entire burden was on Shug to do the moving. Shug was happy with the little three bedroom house. She would always say, it's what you make of it, which we can turn it into a home. Jack and McChella were happy they still had their same friends and were able to go to the same school. Shug's friends were close by also.

Now at this time, Haman hasn't change at all. If anything he got worse. Every time Shug had to go to work she would cry. Not because she was leaving that no good Haman, but leaving her children. It came a time when Shug had to leave home for two months to drive for Greyhound. Shug had to go to work in Knoxville, Tennessee at the Worlds Fair. She was able to come home on weekends, which was good, because she was able see and spend time with her children and take them shopping for clothes. Shug also had something else waiting for her when she got home. Yes, a beating. Haman accused Shug of having a man in Knoxville. Every time Shug left it was heart breaking. But she knew what she had to do and why. Shug had one assurance that eased her guilt of leaving. She knew Haman would not have the opportunity to beat or abuse her emotionally or physically. Driving was the only thing on Shug's mind, and it made her life easier for both her and the children. She would watch other families and it seemed they were happy. But, were the women going through the same thing, just not showing it in public?

Shug did her tour in Knoxville, Tennessee and was headed home. She dreaded it, not for the children but, for that no good Haman. She arrived in Fayetteville, North Carolina, but Haman was not there.

Shug was happy in a way, but she wanted to see her children. As Shug looked around she saw Haman and the children. Of course, he was drunk looking down right stupid. Above all, he had the nerve to try and kiss Shug with his stinking breath. Now, if you know Shug, you could image what she said to herself, give it a rest honey. Pew, you stink. Although she thought this in her head, she dared to say it out loud, in fear of getting slapped in front of the children. After they arrived home, Shug had plenty of time to spend with the children. She was able to cook, clean, and be an at home mom again for awhile. As time went by, Greyhound contacted Shug. They wanted to know if she was interesting in working somewhere else or if she just wantèd to take the furlough. Shug decided to take the furlough and collect the unemployment while spending time with her family. Oh yeah, that included Haman too. Haman was still working and still very abusive. Every day he came home, he would ask Shug questions about being in Knoxville. He asked where she lived and who she lived with. Haman said to Shug, I know you had sex with someone while you were in Knoxville. Shug replied, saying, who had the time to think of that. I was driving buses around the clock. What woman in her right mind wanted another Haman in her bed? She wanted to say more but, she knew what would happen if she did. Haman would look at her with the devil in his eyes, and without warning he would slap Shug across the face. Shug knew not to question him, or she would get another slap. Shug would go on with whatever she was doing, bruised, sore face and all.

Bedtime was another horror story. Shug wondered, what could she do to avoid this, absolutely, nothing. She would wait until Haman went to sleep, then she would sneak into bed. Now, that's horrible. That is not how a marriage should be. But you know as well as I do, this was no normal marriage. As Shug would get into bed, the devil himself would turn over and want to have sex. Haman forced Shug to have sex with him, saying if you don't have sex with me, I'm going to hurt you. He would take his fingernails and dig into her buttocks, causing her to do the right thing. This was a painful ordeal for Shug. But, she had no other choice. In fear of her children being in the next room, she didn't want Haman to start beating her. After the task was over, Shug felt dirty and nasty, so she would go and wash the filth off of her. The next morning Haman got ready for work. This time Shug did not get up to make coffee for him as she had in the past. She would just lie in the bed and pretend to be asleep. Once Haman let the house, Shug got up and made coffee and got the children ready for school. When the children left for school, Shug sat there and wondered. What could she do to make things better for her and the children? At this point, she could only image what life would be like, without someone beating and draining her emotionally.

Shug had a lot of unpacking to do still. As Shug began to unpack, she thought about everything that really didn't matter at that time. Until this day, I wonder what Shug was really thinking about. The hours went by really fast. It was almost time for the children to come home from school. Shug knew she didn't take anything out for dinner, so she made a mad rush to the store to get something. Jack and McChella came home and Shug was happy to see them. McChella asked Shug, when was cheerleading and football practice again? I told her, I will check on that tomorrow. She also wanted to know if she could bring a friend with her. Shug asked, to come a cheerleader? She said yes. I told her it would be alright just as long as her mother gives her permission. Jack would say something to the effect, okay I want to see this, two silly girls going to cheer with his finger in his mouth. Then Jack would laugh. Shug told them to start on their homework while she cooked dinner. Jack asked, what's for dinner? Shug asked him, what do you want? Jack told Shug and she began to laugh, saying, well honey, we won't be having that. We are having fried chicken, rice, corn and maybe a cake. As he sucked on his thumb, he yelled, alright way to go ma. But, are you cooking the rice? Shug answered and said, well yeah, why? Jack just shook his head and walked away. Now remember, Shug couldn't cook that well, and rice was definitely, out of the question. It always came out gummy and sticky. As she prepared dinner, guess who came in the door? That evil person, I called my husband. Shug said, hello Haman, how was your day? He just looked at her, and spoke to the children. Shug said to everyone, dinner would be ready in a few minutes so get washed up. Everyone sat down for dinner, and the children starting talking about their day in school. McChella told Haman mama said, I could bring a friend to cheerleading practice with me. Haman said, that sounds good baby. Jack just sat there. After dinner the children went into the den to watch television for a while with Haman. Shug cleaned up the kitchen. After the children went to bed, Shug sat with Haman and watched the news. Haman asked Shug, are you going to be a cheerleader coach again? Shug said yes, I really enjoy helping out in any way I can. To Shug's surprise Haman was okay with that. Haman said, let's get ready for bed. Shug said, oh lord. She had to come up with something, a headache, cramps or something. Shug had a peaceful sleep not having to deal with Haman. The next morning she thought, if only, I can tell him that every night, I could sleep better.

The next day Shug called the football coach to see if there was going to be football and cheerleading practice. The coach responded by saying, why yes. He asked Shug, are you planning to be the cheerleader coach again this year? Shug said, yes if they would have me. He said yes, yes,

yes, of course. When Jack and McChella came home she told them the news. McChella had already brought her friend Brittany home with her. Can Brittany come, asked McChella? Shug said, I have to ask her mother first. Shug made a phone call to Brittany's mother. Her mother wanted to know if she could come along also. Shug said, by all means please come, so you can meet the other parents. Practice was a good way of getting out of the house, and being with her children, this made her day. After practice, Shug took Jack and McChella to get some ice cream.

Shug had not prepared dinner, and didn't realize the time. She knew she could put something together fast. When Haman came home the children couldn't wait to tell him about practice. He sat and talked with them for awhile. Then he approached Shug and asked her about dinner. She explained, it will be ready in a few minutes. After dinner when the children had gone to bed, Haman began fussing and beating on Shug, telling her he wanted his dinner ready when he get home.

The next day at practice, Shug was hurting so bad from the beating the night before. She was bruised and sore all over, but she didn't want anyone to know. Shug always kept a smile on her face regardless. The girls had to practice because the game was the next day, and Shug wanted them to look good.

The big day, McChella and Jack was so excited. They didn't know the night before, Haman told Shug he didn't want her to drive, that he would attend the game and take them all home.

Haman came to the game drunk, loud acting like a **PURE "T" FOOL.** Jack and McChella looked at Shug and the other parents. Shug never said a word. Although, Jack already knew his father was drunk, he still played his best. After the game, everyone left the ball field. Shug refused to ride in the car with Haman because he was drunk, Shug and the children starting walking toward home. Haman tried to run over Shug by driving the car off the road and then pulling the car back on the road. This happened many of times. People passing by asked Shug if she was alright. She smiled and said, yes, thank you. Shug told Jack and McChella just to keep looking forward. Jack asked, is daddy trying to hit us? I told him, no baby, just keep walking. Now, Shug already knew what kind of night she was in for. Once Shug got home, she saw that the car was not in the yard. Boy, oh boy was she glad. Shug got the children inside, fed them and then told them to get ready for bed. After several hours passed, Haman finally came home, telling her he went to his friend's house. Shug said to herself, why didn't you stay there? Not long after Haman got in the house once again, he started to beat on Shug. He said I saw you looking at this man at the ballpark. I know that was why you wanted to be the cheerleader coach. Shug asked, what are you talking about now? She said it is always something with you. He slapped Shug in the face, threw her into the wall and punched her until Shug actually got tired. That night he wanted Shug to have sex. He already knew she did not want to after he beat her so badly. He took a knife to bed and he put it to Shug's neck. The blade went down her neck and the blood began to trickle down. He told her not to move her body or he would cut her. Shug did not move in fear he would follow through with what he said.

Finally, it was Saturday and there was no school. Shug was so thankful because she could hardly get out of the bed. She was in so much pain, she didn't want the children see her that way. Once Shug went into the bathroom and saw her face, all she could do was sob. Her eyes were black and blue, and she saw where Haman scratched her neck with the knife. Shug just went back to bed and told the children she was going to rest all day. Jack knew something was wrong. He came in to the room and asked Shug if she was alright. She said yes. Did daddy beat you again, asked Jack? Shug told him to be quiet, gave him a big old juicy kiss and told him she loved him, and one day they would all be free to live again.

Chapter 11

Who's sleeping in Shug's Bed?

Shug was called back to work driving for Grey hound once again. She had to work out of Richmond Virginia. This would take her away from home again. Shug didn't like the idea of leaving her children, but she had no other choice. She knew Haman would take good care of them. This was in the summer and the children were out for their summer break. Shug was glad about that, because it would allow the children to be able to ride with her from time to time. When Haman found out she was going to work out of Richmond, he said that was good, because she would be driving to Fayetteville often, and she would be able to come home and stay frequently. Shug enjoyed driving. It would take her mind off the beatings and emotional abuse from Haman. Some of her co-workers would ask her how has she been since furlough, and she replied, I don't even want to talk about it. I'm just glad to be back at work. Shug took as many runs as she could to Fayetteville to spend time with her children. At times she would take the children back with her to Richmond. The children would stay with Shug's friends Rusty and Arvis. Shug was so happy to have her children with her. She even took off the next day to spend time with them. She received a call from work the next evening, to go to New York. The children were so happy they couldn't wait to go. The trip was long, but the children didn't mind al all. They went to sleep, woke back up and went to sleep again. Upon arriving to the City, Shug took off and took the children sight seeing. They had so much fun it brought tears to Shug's eyes. Shug had to get some rest for the drive back to Richmond. Once Shug arrived in Richmond, she took the same bus to Fayetteville to take the children back home for a couple of weeks. Haman met them at the bus station. He was someone Shug did not want to see, but after all he's the children's daddy. We all went to the house, and Haman asked Shug when she was leaving again? She replied, tomorrow. Haman said, well, I guess we can enjoy the night together. Shug said what! The children came into the living room to tell Haman all about their trip. All he wanted to know was, if their mother had a man with her. The children looked at Haman as if he was crazy. They said, no daddy. Jack and McChella were so excited and happy they could barely tell Haman about their trip to New York. They said, daddy, we had so much fun we can't tell it all. While they were talking to Haman, Shug took a bath and went to bed, hoping Haman would sit and talk with the children for a couple of hours.

As weeks went by, Shug was headed for another furlough. She could either take the furlough or to work some place else. Shug needed the money, so she decided to go to Ashland, Kentucky. Shug came home for a week before reporting to Ashland. Haman on the other hand, thought Shug was lying, until he saw the letter. That night, Haman was very ugly to Shug. He began to call her all kinds of names, slapped her, and of course, his favorite, sex. Shug left for Ashland the next day with a knot on her forehead. You might know how it got there. Going to a new and different city to work is hard on anyone, especially if it's their first time. My first thought would be, what is this place like, and will I stay? When Shug arrived in Ashland she had to do a ride alone and learn the route. As you well know, Ashland is a coal miner's town. Shug took off for her first run the next day. I thought, man, oh man, were the miners tall. They actually had to duck as they entered the bus, but they were very nice people. Shug called home to speak with the children. She always asked how their day was going. Shug always expressed to them how much she loved them. She never forgot to tell them. Shug worked through her time in Ashland. She got bumped, meaning another driver had more seniority, so she decided to go home instead of going to working some where else. Shug didn't tell Haman she was coming home just as yet.

The next morning, Shug took the next bus out for Fort Bragg NC. When she arrived at Fort Bragg it was late at night. She decided to take a cab home instead of waking up Haman and the children. When Shug arrived home, she tried to open the door, but it was locked. Shug said to herself, that's strange. So she rung the bell and Haman asked who is it? Shug said it's me, all of a sudden Haman yelled out **OH MY GOD!** Shug couldn't understand why he would say that. As he opened the door, he stepped out to pick up Shug's luggage and took it in the house. When Shug walked into the house she noticed the furniture was rearranged, and she also notice a brown paper bag sitting in on of the chairs. That really didn't matter to Shug at this time she wanted to see her children. Shug walked into Jack's room and woke him up with a kiss. Jack said, hi mom, you're home. Where is daddy? Shug told him he was in the living room and to go back to sleep. Then Shug went McChella's room. She noticed there was a little girl in the bed with McChella. She figures it was one of her friends spending a night over. Shug woke McChella with a kiss also. McChella said, hi mama. Where is daddy? She told her he's in the living room go back to sleep. Now, who was sleeping in Shug's bed? Shug went into the living room to ask Haman what is going on here. By this time, this woman walks out of the bedroom into the kitchen with Shug's gown on shaking and trembling. Now let me tell you who this lady was. If you recall, remember, the lady that came to Shug's house on Christmas Eve in 1980 and cursed Shug out? Yes honey, it was her. Shug told Haman he needed to get dressed and take this woman and her child out of her house. Haman was the type of man you better not tell him what to do. Haman asked Shug, what did you say? Shug looked at him and said, you need to get dressed and get this woman and her child out of my house. To Shug's surprise, Haman just looked at her, and got up and went into the bedroom and got dressed. Once Haman left Jack went to Shug hugged her and said, mommy it's going to be alright. She looked at him and smiled, gave him a kiss and said, thank you and I love you. Now, please go back to bed. McChella on the other hand, wanted to know where her daddy was going. Shug wanted to say something but she just told McChella to please go back to bed, and I love you too.

Once Shug got the children back to bed, she sat there wondering, what in the world just happened. Shug was so upset. All she could do was make herself a cup of coffee and wonder what in the world was she going to do. Now, what do you think? Did she go to her bed where she found the other woman, or just sat there wondering, if she should kill both of them? Shug thought, what in the world would happen to her children if she did that? Shug just sipped on her coffee, thinking to herself, tomorrow is another day. Oh, by the way, she went to sleep on the couch, still saying to herself, I should have killed them both. The next day Shug realized she had to get herself another bed, and she did. Shug found out one of friends was getting rid of a king size bed. Shug asked her if she could buy it? Shug was always there when her friend needed her. She told Shug no, you can't buy it, but you can have it. Shug was so happy to get this bed all she could think of was, what a good night's sleep she was going to get that night.

After several days passed guess who came to the house. You got it, Haman, the nasty buzzard. He used his old key to open the door. Shug was in the other room and didn't hear that buzzard. She came out of the room with a look on her face, which said, if looks could kill he would have died today. Shug asked him, what are you doing here? That no good buzzard had the nerve to say, this is my house and I'm coming home. Shug looked at him and told him he needed to leave. He had the nerve to ask, where am I going? Shug told him, to hell if you are not careful. Now, remember how abusive Haman is. But at this point, Shug really could care less. I think Shug was just hoping Haman would hit her at this point. I believe she would have killed that fool that day. Haman gathered some of his clothes and as he was walking toward the back door, Shug told him to leave the house keys on the dryer. He left he keys as he was leaving and laughing at the same time. As Haman got into his car, Shug was sitting in the living room saying to herself, no, no, oh no, I can't let that no good buzzard get away with this. Shug yelled out to Haman, wait, I have something for you. That nasty no good buzzard was sitting in the car with a smirk on face. She grabbed a two liter coke bottle, walked over to the car and told Haman this is for you. She busted his window out of the car, and told him to get that piece of junk out of her driveway. She told him he needs to thank God everyday he remains alive. Now, can you image what Haman the buzzard looked like okay. I will leave that for your imagination.

Chapter 12

He's Baaaccckkkkkk!

Shug and the children were getting along just fine. Although, they had some money problems, they still knew how to have fun without any fighting and arguing in the house. Shug had a peace of mind. Shug recalls the time the children came home asking mama what's for dinner? Shug replied saying pinto beans and rice. The next day, Jack wanted to know what was for dinner. Again, Shug replied rice and pinto beans. Jack said that's what we had last night. Shug said, no honey we had pinto beans and rice. Jack asked, what's the difference? Shug said, the beans are on the rice this time. Now McChella wanted to know why they haven't had any cake. Shug told her, when you come home tomorrow you will have a cake McChella. Now that Haman gone, Shug wanted her children to have the same thing they had when Haman was there. Remember the Jiffy mix? Shug didn't have any cake mix, so she used the only thing she had; corn bread mix and chocolate icing. So Shug made a cake. When the children came home, again Jack asked, what's for dinner? He said, oh I know, rice and pinto beans. Shug said no, pinto beans, rice and chocolate cake. McChella said yes, I can't wait. McChella rushed to eat her food so she could have some cake. As Shug was cut the cake, she began to laugh to herself as she passed the cake over to McChella and Jack. McChella took a big bite and said this isn't cake. This is cornbread with chocolate icing. Jack said it's okay mama. McChella said, no its not, but she still ate it. After dinner the three of them sat and talked a little while watching television. Once the children went to bed, Shug sat there wondering what she should do next.

The next day after the children went to school, Shug heard a car pulling in her yard. She got up from the table wondering, who in the world could this be? Well, it was that no good nasty buzzard, Haman. Shug asked, what in the world could he possibly want? Haman asked Shug if he could come in. As she opened the door, she wondered if he would start an argument or if he came to say he was sorry. What do you want, Shug asked? He said, I'm coming back home. I want to be with my children, and no one is going to stop me from doing just that. Now on the other hand, Shug was wondering if he was going to say he was sorry for bringing that woman into her home. Guess what, he never did even until today. Shug asked him, what are you planning to do? Do you think it's right for you to have another woman in our home? Haman just looked at Shug as if to say, be for real. Haman turned and said, I'm going to the car to get my things. Shug pondered in her mind, what should she do? She felt deep inside, she could stab him to death and get away with it, or could she could fix him something to eat and put some rat poison or roach spray in it. Shug really had to think about that. She knew she was not raised to hate people, or do any physical harm to them. She thought to herself, but he's not a person he's an animal. Shug watched Haman as he brought his things into the house. Shug asked Haman if he would like a cup of coffee. He said, that would be nice, thank you. Shug thought to herself; don't thank me now, you might not be able to drink the entire cup. Shug said, oh no honey, don't even think about it. As Haman sat down to drink his coffee, Shug just looked at him. He wanted to know how the children were doing. Shug said, you can see for yourself when they come home. Haman wanted to know what was for dinner. Shug looked at him and asked, did you bring anything with you? She said maybe you should have stayed where ever you were to have dinner instead of coming here. Haman said, here you mean home, don't you?

The door swung open with loud screams. Shug came running out of the bedroom to see what was going on. McChella was filled with joy to see her daddy. On the other hand, Jack wasn't excited at all. Jack asked Shug, is daddy back to stay? Shug said, yes he is. Jack replied, oh man. Shug realized that Jack was not happy with Haman's return. Jack remembered what Haman done to his mother over the years. He remembered the abuse. In a child's eyes that can be hurtful and harmful. Shug told Jack to always respect your father. All Jack could do was look at Haman and walk away.

Now Haman has been at the house for awhile now. No, the abuse had not stopped. But now, Haman was not physically abusive but emotionally. Looking back now, I would rather he hit me instead. Emotional abuse is the worst, because the words cut deeper than any wounds ever could. Haman drinking got worst, he never stopped or tried to stop. He would invite both his friends and girlfriends over and they would sit and drink as long as they wanted to. Shug would just sit there and wonder what in the world are those nasty hussies thinking of me. Shug also wondered if they were in my house when she wasn't home. Shug wanted to speak out but, but was afraid of what Haman would say or do.

Now, do you remember the tramp that was sleeping in Shug's bed? Well, let me tell you something, he brought the tramp back to Shug's house once again. Now any other woman would say, what in the hell are you doing man, are you crazy? Shug just stood there in the door wondering, what in the world is this? Not only did he bring her, he also brought his friend and his girlfriend. The tramp looked at Shug as if to say, what are you going to say now? Shug asked Haman to come into the bedroom. She wanted to know what was going on. He ignorantly answered, nothing, and went back to his company. Shug stayed in the bedroom, feeling worst than fool. Haman decided to take his company and leave. He told Shug, I'll be back later, and everyone burst out laughing.

Haman came home the next day. Shug told him he needed to leave. How dare you bring your whore in this house? Not once, but twice. What did I say that for? He began to beat Shug again punching her like a man. Don't you tell me who to bring in this house, and she is not a whore. If you know what's good for you, you better not call her that again.

The next day Shug decided to pack her things and leave Haman. After all, she had a good job, and she didn't need a man to take care of her. As she was packing her mother's china, she broke down, wishing her mother and father were there. Shug took a break to have some coffee. As she sat there, she said to herself, I know mother you told me not to marry him. I wish I had listened to you. I miss you both so very much. Shug came to realize, when you lose your mother, you have lost your best friend. Whoever is reading this and your mother is still alive, please call her and let her know how much you love her. Give her flowers while she can see and smell them, because once she is gone, she's gone.

While she was packing she called a good friend to ask, if she would store some of her things in her house until she get settled? Her friend replied, yes, of course. She wanted to know what was going on, Shug told her she was leaving Haman. Her friend said, thank God, it's about time. Shug packed a lot of things, and was happy with her decision. Shug knew Jack was fine with her decision. McChella on the other hand, was not. But Shug couldn't think about that at this time. Shug went to the back room to get some more stuff. All of a sudden, Haman walked into the house. What are you doing or where do you think you are going? Shug told him, I'm leaving you. I have taken all of your beatings and name calling, but I will not live with you and you continue to bring your whores in this house anytime you want. Haman said, you think you are going to leave me? Well watch this. Haman lifted four boxes up and dropped them all on the floor. Then he started to fight Shug. Haman threw Shug down on the floor and began to strangle her. Shug thought she was dead for sure. Then a friend came to the door and stopped Haman from killing her. Until this day, she always wondered, had her friend not come to the door, would she be alive today?

The next day, Haman was sitting around drunk, looking like a pure T fool. Haman looked at Shug, asking her what happened to you? I guess you can imagine what Shug looked like. While Shug sat drinking her coffee Haman asked, will you make me a cup of coffee? Shug got up, thinking, this is my chance to kill him. I can put something in his coffee and no one would know the difference. Or, I can wait until he goes to bed and bust his head wide open. Oh no, she thought. The children are here. Meanwhile, Haman is using the bathroom. When he came out, he smeared his bowel movement on the wall and grabbed Shug and rubbed it all over her face. Now, what kind of man would do that to the mother of his children, or the woman he confesses to love? Haman started beating Shug again. At this time, Jack was twelve years old. He jumped between them and told Haman, if you hit my mother again, I **WILL KILL YOU WITH MY BARE HANDS.** He lifted his hands and shook them in his face. Shug looked at Jack and saw the rage in his eyes. Shug knew he meant what he said. She knew then she had to do something quick. She could not have her son go to jail for the rest of his life for killing his father. That was Shug's final straw.

Chapter 13

Free at Last

In the chapter 12, you read how Jack told Haman that he would kill him if he continued to beat his mother. Shug could not let that happen. Shug prayed and prayed, asking God to help her. The next day, Shug received a letter in the mail from Greyhound wanting to know where she wanted to work. The choice was Fayetteville, North Carolina, Richmond Virginia, or New York City. Shug wanted to get as far away as she could from Haman. So she volunteered to work in New York. She called her supervisor and they told her she would get a letter in the mail when to report. Oh thank you, Lord, she yelled. Shug called her cousin in New York and told him the good news. He was so happy that she was finally getting away from that evil devil.

When Haman came home that night Shug told him the news. Haman looked at Shug and told her she was not leaving with the children. She told him, oh yes I am. Haman said, well you "B" I will kill you first. Shug sat up all night wondering what in the world was she going to do. She finally decided to tell Haman she was going to leave the children there with him. Shug had to tell Jack and McChella. Well, I think you already know what McChella said. I want to stay with my daddy. Shug told Jack if I try to take you he will try to kill me or hurt me enough to put me in the hospital. Jack was a sweet child. He said to Shug, I know how you must feel mommy. Jack wanted to know from his daddy if they would be able to see Shug again. Shug said, why yes, weekends, holidays and for vacation. After hearing that, Jack had the biggest smile on his face you ever wanted to see.

The day finally came when Shug left, crying of course. Leaving her children was the most hurtful thing she ever did. Leaving that Haman was joy and a half. As Shug left the house she began to shout, free at last, free at last!

This particular morning as she got dressed for work, she got a call from Haman. Shug didn't want to answer the phone, but she thought something might be wrong with Jack or McChella. Are the children ok, she asked? He said yes, nothing to that affect. He informed Shug he was coming to New York to kill her. Shug asked him, what did you say? He said, you heard me "B". I'm coming there just to kill you. Shug worried all day and night. You see, Haman could ride the bus free of charge because everyone knew he was Shug's husband. Shug knew he would follow through with his promise as far as killing her. She called the Richmond, Virginia dispatcher to ask him if he was riding the bus. Shug couldn't sleep at all that night. The next day, a good friend of

Shug's asked, why don't you call to see if he is still there? You know, you might be right, said Shug. She made the call, and to her surprise, Haman answered the phone. Shug exhaled and released a huge sigh of relief.

After several months, Shug decided to get a divorce from Haman. That day came when Shug found herself to be a divorced woman shouting from the top of her voice,

<u>FREE AT LAST, FREE AT LAST THANK GOD ALMIGHTY I'M FREE AT LAST!!!</u>